In 1910, when this photograph was taken, Flagg was living on 67th Street in a studio-apartment furnished with 16th century acquisitions made in Florence. A portrait of Nellie hangs on the far wall. Flagg worked from professional models and draped mannequins. Courtesy Everett Raymond Kinstler.

THE JAMES MONTGOMERY FLAGG POSTER BOOK

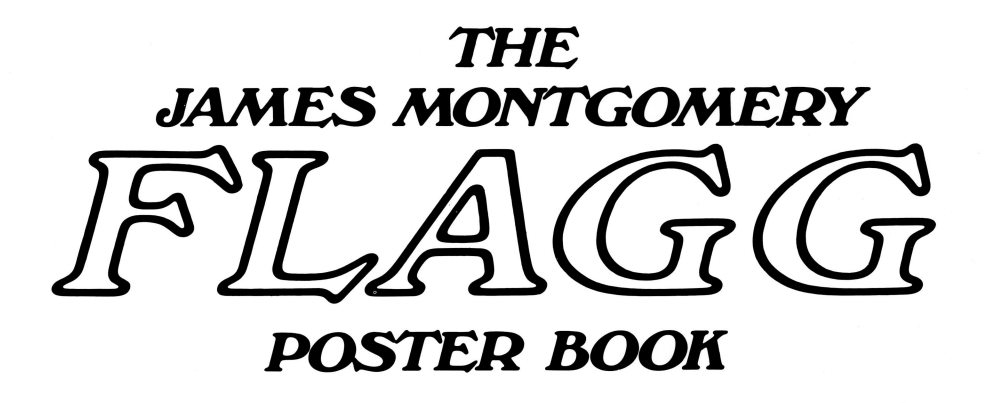

WITH AN INTRODUCTION BY SUSAN E. MEYER

WATSON-GUPTILL PUBLICATIONS/NEW YORK

Manufactured in U.S.A.

ISBN 0–8230–1836–9

Library of Congress Catalog Card Number: 74–25890

First Printing, 1975

INTRODUCTION

James Montgomery Flagg was not only an artist of his time, but a participant in the life he depicted. His life and work form a composite portrait of America. He captured the spirit and personality of the first half of this century in his illustrations, in his writings, in his films, and in the way he lived. He was not only America's most popular illustrator, but he was also its most conspicuous bohemian.

Today Flagg is remembered more for his poster "I Want You" than for any other achievement of his career. Strange as it may seem, this artist whose work was exhibited every week in all the major publications was made immortal by this single poster, a minute fraction of his total output. Yet if he is to be remembered for any one thing, this poster is the most obvious selection. Originally drawn for the cover of *Leslie's Weekly*, "I Want You" was to become the most famous poster of both world wars, an estimated four million copies issued in the first World War and about 400,000 in the second.

Formerly a benign old man in stars and stripes, Uncle Sam was transformed by Flagg into a compelling leader who meant business. Never again would Uncle Sam be regarded in quite the old manner.

Flagg's ink and wash posters of World War One were widely circulated. Cloaked in white robes or in stars and stripes, the Flagg girls now represented America itself: seductive and courageous, proud and hopeful.

Flagg's posters for World War Two reflected the tastes and mood of the 40s as his World War One posters had reflected the teens: splashy, contrived paintings had replaced the satirical, decorative pen and ink washes. This was the temper of the times, and the fatigue of the great illustrator. Flagg was already 64 when the United States entered the second war.

But during World War One, Flagg and his poster art were at their peak. During that time, The New York Public Library on 42nd Street became the forum for publicity campaigns. A crowd would gather on the steps to watch the artists paint recruitment posters; entertainers came to perform on the steps; thousand-dollar Liberty Bonds were sold in exchange for portrait drawings. It was on these steps that Flagg painted "Tell that to the Marines," a phrase that had previously implied the Marines would believe anything. The powerful man removing his jacket for battle in Flagg's poster transformed this insulting phrase into a battle cry.

On these same steps—Flagg himself, recalls in his autobiography—that he and the actress Frances Starr had to introduce each other.

"If you'll say I'm America's greatest actress," she whispered, "I'll say you are America's greatest artist!"

THE POSTERS

I Want You, *1918. Collection Library of Congress.*

WAKE UP, AMERICA !

CIVILIZATION CALLS
EVERY MAN WOMAN AND CHILD !
MAYOR'S COMMITTEE 50 EAST 42ND ST

Wake Up America! *ca. 1918. Collection Library of Congress.*

SIDE BY SIDE~
BRITANNIA!

James Montgomery Flagg. 1918.

Britain's Day Dec. 7th 1918

MASS MEETING

Side By Side, Britannia! *1918. Collection Library of Congress.*

travel?
adventure?
answer – Join the Marines!
ENLIST TO-DAY FOR 2-3 OR 4 YEARS

JAMES MONTGOMERY FLAGG

Travel? Adventure? ca. 1918. Collection of Naval Academy Museum, Annapolis, Md.

FIRST IN
THE FIGHT~

ALWAYS
FAITHFUL~

BE A U.S. MARINE !

First in the Fight, Always Faithful, *ca. 1918. Collection Library of Congress.*

JAMES MONTGOMERY FLAGG

TOGETHER WE WIN

UNITED STATES SHIPPING BOARD   ISSUED BY PUBLICATIONS SECTION EMERGENCY FLEET CORPORATION PHILADELPHIA, PA.   EMERGENCY FLEET CORPORATION

Together We Win, *ca. 1918. Collection Library of Congress.*

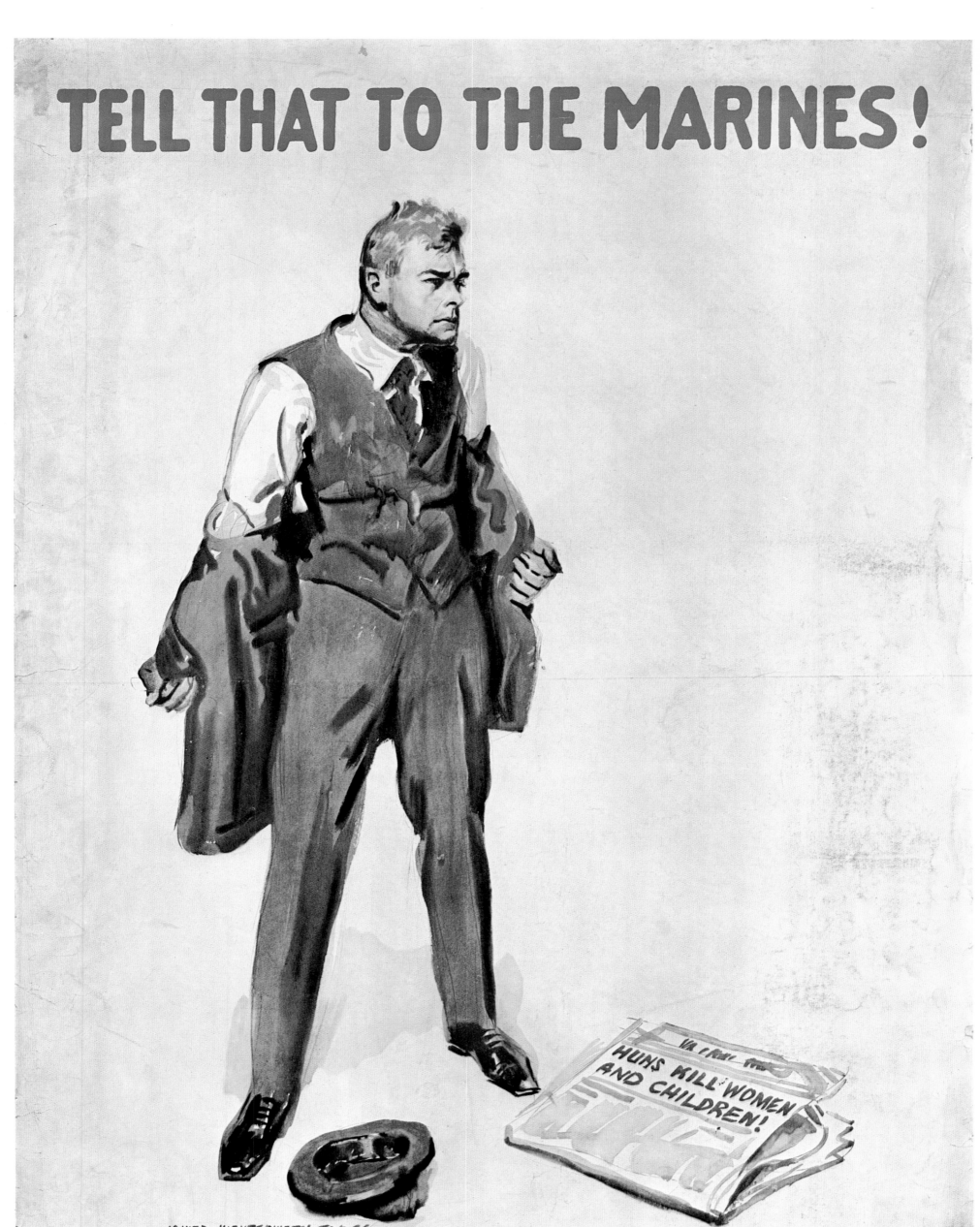

Tell That to the Marines, *1918. Collection Library of Congress.*

Wake Up America Day, *1917. Collection Library of Congress.*

The Navy Needs You, *1918. Collection Library of Congress.*

BOYS and GIRLS!
You can Help your Uncle Sam
Win the War

W.S.S.

W.S.S.
WAR SAVINGS STAMPS
ISSUED BY THE
UNITED STATES
GOVERNMENT

Save your Quarters
BUY WAR SAVINGS STAMPS

Boys and Girls! You Can Help, *1918. Collection Library of Congress.*

Will you have a part in Victory?

WRITE TO THE
NATIONAL
WAR GARDEN
COMMISSION ~
WASHINGTON, D.C.
for free books on
gardening, canning
& drying.

© 1918 · NATIONAL WAR GARDEN COMMISSION

JAMES MONTGOMERY FLAGG

"Every Garden a Munition Plant"

Charles Lathrop Pack, President

Will You Have a Part in Victory? *1918. Collection Library of Congress.*

Hold On to Uncle Sam's Insurance, *1918. Collection Library of Congress.*

Stage Women's War Relief, *1918. Collection Library of Congress.*

ALL FOR ONE AND ONE FOR ALL!
VIVE LA FRANCE!

JAMES MONTGOMERY FLAGG

Allied Tribute to France: July 14, at 5 p.m.

MASS MEETING on the French National Holiday
to show we all stand together till we win Peace by Victory

Vive La France, *ca. 1918. Collection Library of Congress.*

OUR REGULAR DIVISIONS

JAMES MONTGOMERY FLAGG

Honored and Respected by All
Enlist for the Infantry—
or in one of the other 12 branches.

Nearest Recruiting Office :

Our Regular Divisions, Honored and Respected by All, *1918. Collection Library of Congress.*

HELP CHINA!

JAMES MONTGOMERY FLAGG

CHINA IS HELPING US
UNITED CHINA RELIEF

Help China, *ca. 1944. Collection Library of Congress.*

Coming Right Up!

Coming Right Up! *1945. Collection Library of Congress.*

Want Action? Join U.S. Marine Corps, *1942. Collection Library of Congress.*

The Marines Have Landed, *1942. Collection Library of Congress.*

Your Red Cross Needs You, *1942. Collection Library of Congress.*